BUILD4SKILLS
PRACTICE GUIDE FOR PROCUREMENT PRACTITIONERS

SEPTEMBER 2024

ASIAN DEVELOPMENT BANK

ADB

© 2024 Asian Development Bank
6 ADB Avenue, Mandaluyong City, 1550 Metro Manila, Philippines
Tel +63 2 8632 4444; Fax +63 2 8636 2444
www.adb.org

Some rights reserved. Published in 2024.

ISBN 978-92-9270-903-7 (print); 978-92-9270-904-4 (PDF); 978-92-9270-905-1 (ebook)
Publication Stock No. TIM240450-2
DOI: http://dx.doi.org/10.22617/TIM240450-2

The views expressed in this publication are those of the authors and do not necessarily reflect the views and policies of the Asian Development Bank (ADB) or its Board of Governors or the governments they represent.

ADB does not guarantee the accuracy of the data included in this publication and accepts no responsibility for any consequence of their use. The mention of specific companies or products of manufacturers does not imply that they are endorsed or recommended by ADB in preference to others of a similar nature that are not mentioned.

By making any designation of or reference to a particular territory or geographic area in this document, ADB does not intend to make any judgments as to the legal or other status of any territory or area.

Please contact pubsmarketing@adb.org if you have questions or comments with respect to content, or if you wish to obtain copyright permission for your intended use that does not fall within these terms, or for permission to use the ADB logo.

Corrigenda to ADB publications may be found at http://www.adb.org/publications/corrigenda.

Note:
In this publication, "$" refers to United States dollars.

Cover design by Cleone Baradas.

Contents

Tables, Figure, and Box   iv

Acknowledgments   v

Purpose of the Practice Guide   vi

Introduction: What Are Traineeship Contract Requirements?   1

How to Integrate Traineeships into Civil Work Contracts of ADB Investment Projects   3

     Overall Process and Key Roles and Responsibilities   3

     Suitability Assessment for Build4Skills Traineeships   4

     Market Engagement Survey for Build4Skills Traineeships   5

     Setting Traineeship Requirements   5

     Incorporating Traineeships Requirements into Bidding Documents   6

     Incorporating a Provisional Sum for Traineeships in the Bill of Quantities   6

     Managing Provisional Sums and Disbursements   10

     Verify quality of traineeship delivery in detail   12

Appendixes

   1   Traineeship Specifications to Be Included in Bidding Documents   14

   2   Template for Market Survey for Traineeships   18

   3   Trainee Evaluation Form Template   20

Tables, Figure, and Box

Tables

1	Criteria to Determine Build4Skills Suitability of Civil Works Contract Packages	5
2	Bill of Quantities Example for Bidding Document	7
3	Two Approaches to Calculating Provisional Sum and Trainee Targets	7
4	Determining Percentage to Be Earmarked for Traineeships Based on Total Civil Works Contract Values	8
5	Disbursement Plan (Monthly Disbursements)	11
6	Build4Skills Quality Checklist Before Traineeship Start	12
7	Definitions of Noncompliance for Key Traineeship Specifications	13

Figure

Considering Traineeships Requirement Throughout the ADB Procurement Cycle	3

Box

Can Other Types of Traineeship Arrangements be Promoted?	2

Acknowledgments

The publication was prepared by Alexander Tsironis, education specialist at the Human and Social Development Sector Office of the Asian Development Bank.

Special thanks are extended to Kevin Moore, principal procurement specialist; Jenny Yan Yee Chu, procurement specialist; and Prasath Sanjeewa, procurement specialist, at the Procurement, Portfolio, and Financial Management Department for their substantial contributions and commitment to driving the knowledge work forward. Additional thanks are extended to Philipp Kalpaxis, senior procurement specialist at Procurement, Portfolio, and Financial Management Department, for peer reviewing the publication.

Support in the finalization of this publication was provided by Asian Development Bank colleagues Dorothy Geronimo, senior education officer, Sector Group - Human and Social Development and Maria Theresa Mercado, editor (consultant).

Purpose of the Practice Guide

The Asian Development Bank (ADB) has developed the Build4Skills approach to promote traineeships and skills development as part of ADB supported infrastructure projects in the energy, transport, water, urban, and social sector.[1] The approach recommends that ADB- supported infrastructure projects make the delivery of traineeships a requirement in civil work contracts, requiring contractors to provide traineeship[2] opportunities to local youth on construction sites. The underlying idea is that all infrastructure projects can generate wider societal benefits through a simple change to procurement requirements, resulting in significant outcomes for youth and communities including: (i) improving youth's skills and transition into jobs, (ii) connecting contractors to skilled talents from the local labor market, and (iii) enabling ADB clients and partners to enhance a project's inclusiveness and reputation.

The approach is outlined in the *ADB Build4Skills Handbook*, first published in 2023. The handbook describes how ADB investment projects can operationalize Build4Skills traineeships from end-to-end, including client consultations, project processing, and delivery of traineeships. Experience from Build4Skills pilots has shown that in-depth technical guidance on procurement related steps is a critical success factor. Therefore, to complement the handbook, this *Build4Skills Practice Guide for Procurement Practitioners* has been developed. The practice guide zooms into the procurement related steps of the Build4Skills approach. It outlines in detail how procurement specialists and consultants of OneADB teams can incorporate traineeship requirements into bidding documents, calculate traineeship cost estimates to be included in the bill of quantities (BOQ), and manage disbursements during project implementation. In addition, it provides template traineeship requirements and specifications for ease of use. With the practice guide OneADB teams have all the information needed to successfully incorporate traineeships into the project design of ADB infrastructure investment projects. The practice guide was developed by the ADB's Human Social Development Sector Group together with the Procurement, Portfolio, and Financial Management Department.

---

[1] ADB. 2023. *Build4Skills: Integrating Traineeships into ADB Supported Infrastructure Projects*.

[2] The terminologies of traineeships, on-the-job training and work-based training may be used interchangeably. All confer that training takes place at the workplace.

Introduction: What Are Traineeship Contract Requirements?

Why is there an opportunity for traineeships on ADB-supported infrastructure projects?

Build4Skills unlocks the skills development potential of infrastructure investments. The Build4Skills approach is based on the premise that all infrastructure projects can generate work and training opportunities in alignment with the Sustainable Development Goals. In practice, these opportunities are often not intentionally leveraged by infrastructure projects due to a lack of approaches and operational procedures. The *Build4Skills Handbook* and this practice guide addresses this gap by providing a step-by-step procedure on integrating traineeships into project designs and procurement documents, enabling projects to unlock the potential for additional impact. A key advantage of the approach is that it can be easily integrated into any project by simply incorporating traineeship requirements in civil work bidding documents.

Build4Skills is aligned with key ADB and global strategies. The Build4Skills approach aligns with key global as well as ADB strategies and initiatives including (i) ADB Strategy 2030[1] (operational priority [OP] 1–enhanced human capital for all and quality jobs generated, and potentially OP2–enhanced gender equality in human development); (ii) the G20 Quality Infrastructure Investment Principles[2] (principle on social considerations); and (iii) the ADB Sustainable Public Procurement: Guidance Note on Procurement.[3]

What type of traineeships does the Build4Skills approach promote?

Build4Skills promotes a specific type of traineeship. Build4Skills promotes traineeships with the following characteristics: (i) short-term (6–12 weeks); (ii) quality driven; (iii) in construction-related occupations only;[4] (iv) aimed at local youth, who are enrolled in construction-related technical and vocational education and training (TVET) programs or recent graduates (6 months or less); and (v) incorporated in civil work

---

[1]   ADB. 2022. *Strategy 2030 Education Sector Directional Guide.*
[2]   ADB. 2021. *Supporting Quality Infrastructure in Developing Asia.*
[3]   ADB. 2021. Sustainable Public Procurement: Guidance Note on Procurement.
[4]   Technical jobs include but are not limited to welders, bricklayers, joiners, electrician, painters, pipefitters, roofers, ironworkers, and civil engineers.

contract requirements. These characteristics are intentional to ensure that traineeships can be feasibly implemented as explained in the following paragraphs:

- **Rationale for the time frame (6–12 weeks).** When trainees are still enrolled students in TVET institutes, they often cannot be absent from schools longer than 6–8 weeks. Limiting traineeships periods to 12 weeks also encourages contractors to hire trainees as workers upon satisfactory performance as a trainee.

- **Rationale for age group (youth).** Youth unemployment is a policy challenge in almost all countries. The school-to-work transition is a crucial step for youth to find employment, and youth require targeted support. Build4Skills therefore aims at youth as beneficiaries.

- **Rationale for youth with TVET background.** Construction sites can typically accommodate more TVET-level traineeships than those in the higher education, given sites' workforce composition. In addition, a TVET background ensures that contractors receive trainees who can make reliable and productive contributions and have a level of expertise to perform work tasks safely.

- **Rationale for quality traineeships.** The proposed ADB Environmental and Social Framework[5] highlights that youth, when underage, should not be engaged in a manner that is economically exploitative or likely hazardous or may interfere with the child's education, or may be harmful to the child's health or physical, mental, spiritual, moral, or social development. The Build4Skills approach therefore promotes quality traineeships that (i) are financially and fairly remunerated; (ii) appropriately address occupational health and safety (e.g., provision of personal protective equipment [PPE]); (iii) are educational traineeships, and (iv) are supervised by professional staff of contractors.

- **Rationale for traineeship as a requirement in civil work contracts.** Civil work contracts provide the largest number of traineeship opportunities as they typically contract out the largest economic activities of a project. Other contracts such as consulting contracts tend to involve smaller activities and provide some while typically less traineeship opportunities.

Other types of traineeship arrangements with different characteristics (e.g., longer durations) can in principle also be promoted in ADB infrastructure projects (Box).

Box: Can Other Types of Traineeship Arrangements be Promoted?

Yes, Asian Development Bank (ADB) infrastructure projects can also promote other traineeship arrangements. For example, traineeship as a requirement for engineering supervision consultancy contracts, with a duration of 6 months, aimed at higher education engineering students, is another feasible way to promote traineeships. The Build4Skills approach as presented in this practice guide focuses on vocational education-level traineeships given the outlined rationale. Projects may consider delivering different variants of the Build4Skills approach based on ADB client needs and priorities. These variants are not mutually exclusive.

Source: ADB.

---

5   ADB. 2023. Environmental and Social Framework (consultation draft).

How to Integrate Traineeships into Civil Work Contracts of ADB Investment Projects

Overall Process and Key Roles and Responsibilities

Procurement specialists and consultants consider traineeship requirements throughout a project's procurement cycle. The mechanism by which traineeships are integrated into project designs is through the incorporation of traineeship requirements into civil work bidding documents and contracts. The following pages outline how OneADB teams process Build4Skills traineeships in key steps of the ADB procurement cycle (Figure).

Figure: Considering Traineeships Requirement Throughout the ADB Procurement Cycle

Procurement Planning	Bidding	Bid evaluation and contract award	Contract management Implementation Monitoring
Access suitability of civil works contract packages	Incorporate traineeship requirements into bidding documents	No specific activity, part of regular bid evaluation and contract award	Manage disbursements for traineeships
Define traineeship requirements	Incorporate provisional sum for traineeships into BOQ		Verify quality of traineeship delivery
Conduct market engagement survey (optional)			

BOQ = bill of quantities.
Source: Asian Development Bank.

Employers[6] and contractors have different roles and responsibilities in Build4Skills traineeships. The employer, supported by the OneADB team, makes traineeships a contract requirement for bidders. The employer defines traineeship requirements, monitors if these requirements are met and compliant with contract specifications and manages related disbursements.

The contractor delivers traineeships as per contract requirements and specifications. The delivery of traineeships requires contractors to collaborate with local TVET institutes and students. It is the responsibility of contractors to proactively plan, coordinate (e.g., with TVET institutes), and deliver traineeships. In addition, it is the responsibility of contractors to raise any issues to the employer, before and during traineeship implementation, that may be an obstacle to delivering traineeships.

PROCUREMENT PLANNING

Suitability Assessment for Build4Skills Traineeships

Identifying suitable civil works contract packages for traineeships.[7] During the strategic procurement planning (SPP)[8] process, the OneADB project team, including the assigned ADB procurement staff, identifies the civil work contract packages in the procurement plan that are suitable for integrating traineeships. The suitability is determined by three criteria: (i) estimated civil work contract package size, (ii) duration of a given civil work contract package, and (iii) proximity to TVET institute (Table 1). Information on the first two criteria will be available from the One ADB team. As for the third criterion (proximity of TVET institutes), it can be assumed that if the construction is in urban areas, TVET institutes are located nearby. In rural areas, the choice and availability of institutes shall be discussed with the employer. If the distance between the construction site and TVET institutes cannot be estimated at this stage, Build4Skills may still be considered suitable and shall proceed.

Record suitable contract packages in the SPP report. The ADB project team records the suitable civil work contract packages in the sustainable procurement section of the SPP report.

---

6   The employer can be synonymous with the executing agency, implementing agency, project implementation unit (PIU), including supervision consultants who supports the employer to administer contracts.

7   This activity is equivalent to step 2 in the Build4Skills Handbook.

8   ADB. 2021. _Strategic Procurement Planning: Guidance Note on Procurement_.

Table 1: Criteria to Determine Build4Skills Suitability of Civil Works Contract Packages

Suitability Criteria	Suitable	Not Suitable
The construction duration is longer than 12 months.	Yes	No
The contract price of individual civil work contract package is greater than $500,000.	Yes	No
The construction site is located 30 miles or less from relevant TVET institutes. (If unknown, this criterion can be skipped.)	Yes, or unknown	No
	Contract package is suitable, proceed	Contract package is not suitable

TVET = technical and vocational education and training.
Source: Author.

Market Engagement Survey for Build4Skills Traineeships

Procurement staff may use market engagement to assess market maturity and tailor traineeship requirements to local market conditions. Due to the simplicity of traineeships as an activity, market engagement to verify its capacity for traineeship delivery is not strictly necessary. Project teams can decide on a case-by-case basis if this analysis is needed to further inform the integration of traineeships in the procurement documents. Market maturity for traineeship provisions can be assessed based on (i) existing country knowledge, (ii) desk-based review of industry practices, and/or (iii) a market survey of contractors. TVET institutes may also be used as a source of information in surveys. Insights from the market engagement may be reflected in the traineeship requirements. A template market survey, which can be tailored as needed, is provided in Appendix 2. The outlined questions on traineeships may be included in a general market survey not requiring a separate traineeship-specific survey.

Setting Traineeship Requirements

Defining traineeship requirements. The OneADB team supports the employer in defining traineeship requirements and specifications. Template traineeship requirements are outlined in Appendix 1, which can be directly copied into the technical specifications section of bidding documents. The requirements describe the minimum specifications that contractors shall fulfill to ensure the delivery of quality traineeships. The template requirements in Appendix 1 are formulated to apply to any context.

Tailoring traineeship requirements to context. The requirements in Appendix 1 may be further detailed by the employer to reflect needs and local circumstances such as existing traineeship regulations, construction industry standards, or national labor law. For example, the employer may set specific gender targets, or define which exact occupations traineeships should take place (e.g., electricians, welders etc.). Alternatively, the employer may decide to leave the exact details of traineeship delivery to contractors while setting only a traineeship target and general quality requirements that contractors need to comply with as provided in

Appendix 1. It is recommended that the employer does not reduce or substantially change the suggested requirements (Appendix 1) as they aim to ensure that traineeships are provided at sufficient quality and include social safeguard.

Traineeships are typically not a prequalification requirement as it is a secondary objective being delivered through infrastructure contracts. As traineeships are comparatively simple activities, they can be implemented by contractors even if they have limited prior experience.

BIDDING

Incorporating Traineeships Requirements into Bidding Documents

Traineeship requirements are included in the technical specifications of bidding documents. Traineeship requirements are incorporated in those civil work contract packages that have been identified as suitable in the suitability assessment. The requirements are incorporated in the specification or employer's requirements of bidding documents. There is normally no need to include it additionally as a contract clause. By submitting a bid, contractors commit to fulfilling traineeship specifications in the same way as other binding obligations under the contract. See previous section and Appendix 1 for details on the content of traineeship requirements.

Incorporating a Provisional Sum for Traineeships in the Bill of Quantities

Traineeship costs are included in the BOQ of bidding documents. Traineeship costs are included in the BOQ or equivalent pricing document, normally as a provisional sum. The traineeship requirements and budget are the same for all bidders ensuring that an adequate amount of money is retained to implement the traineeship program. An example BOQ is shown in Table 2 with a traineeship target of 85 trainees and a provisional sum of $54,400, based on an estimated average cost of $640 per 2 months traineeship.

Table 2: Bill of Quantities Example for Bidding Document

Bill no.	Item no. (Specification reference)	Description	Amount in $ (provisional sum, noncompetitive item)
1	Build4Skills 1	Delivery of 85 on-site traineeships for local youth in line with technical specifications	54,400.00

Source: Asian Development Bank.

There are two different approaches to determine the provisional sum and trainee target (quantity) for the BOQ. The employer may use either one of the two outlined approaches in Table 3 to determine the provisional sum and traineeship targets for the BOQ. The examples outlined in Table 3 use different (exemplary) values to demonstrate the calculation behind each approach. They do not relate nor compete with one another.

Table 3: Two Approaches to Calculating Provisional Sum and Trainee Targets

#	Approach	Calculation Steps	Example
1	Trainee Target Led Calculation	1: Employer sets a trainee target (quantity) based on experience. 2: Employer estimates average traineeship cost. 3: Employer multiplies the trainee target by the average trainee cost, resulting in the total provisional sum.	1: 107 trainees 2: $540 3: 107 x $540 = $57,780
2	Earmarked Budget Led Calculation	1: Employer earmarks a given percentage of the value of each civil work package as a lump sum for traineeships. Following the recommended percentages in Table 4, the earmarked percentage, in this example is 0.4% as the combined civil works contract value ($36 million) is in the $31 million–$45 million range. 2: Employer estimates average traineeship cost. 3: Employer Divides the provisional sum by the average trainee cost resulting in the traineeship target.	1: $36 million x 0.4% = $129,600 2: $640 3: $129,600/$640 = 203 trainees

Source: Asian Development Bank.

- **In approach 1, a target is set first.** The employer sets the traineeship target based on their professional experience of what is a feasible and desirable target. Then, the average trainee costs are estimated, which are then multiplied by the traineeship target (Table 3). This calculation results in the estimated budget needed to achieve the traineeship target. Approach 1 may be followed in the context in which employers have experience with traineeships on construction sites that enables them to set realistic targets.

- **In approach 2, a budget is earmarked first.** The employer first earmarks and adds a given percentage of the value of each civil work package as a lump sum for traineeships thereby setting the provisional sum. The percentage to be earmarked for traineeships differs depending on the total value of civil work contract packages that apply Build4Skills traineeships as outlined in Table 4.[9] For example, if the combined value of civil work contract packages that are suitable for the Build4Skills approach is between $31 million–$45 million, it is recommended to add 0.4% of the contract value as a provisional sum in the BOQ in each suitable civil work contract package. Once a budget has been earmarked, the average trainee costs is estimated, and the provisional sum divided through it. This calculation provides a traineeship target estimate.[10] Finally, the employer needs to verify if the given construction site can accommodate the calculated traineeship target. Generally, constructions sites can accommodate numerous traineeships when they are spaced out over the entire construction duration into various traineeship batches. Approach 2 may be followed in the context in which employers have no experience with traineeships and there is no clear basis for setting realistic traineeship targets.

Table 4: Determining Percentage to Be Earmarked for Traineeships Based on Total Civil Works Contract Values

Total value of all civil works contract packages that are suitable to apply the Build4Skills approach	% to be earmarked for traineeships
$10 million–$30 million	0.5
$31 million–$45 million	0.4
$46 million–$69 million	0.3
$70 million–$100 million	0.25
>$100 million	Capped at $250,000

Source: Asian Development Bank.

How average traineeship costs can be estimated. Approaches 1 and 2 as outlined requires OneADB teams to estimate the average traineeship costs. Traineeships involve three eligible cost items: (i) trainee allowance, (ii) workplace injury insurance costs, (iii) PPE costs. Other potential costs related to traineeships (e.g., instructor labor hours, work material, and occupational health and safety training) are not eligible. Those other costs are expected to be marginal and may be incurred by contractors regardless of traineeships. Contractors may incorporate or subsume those other costs in other parts of their bids. A rigorous approach to the eligibility of traineeship expenses aims to ensure that contractors do not misappropriate the traineeship budget for other or only marginally related expenses. To realistically estimate the costs for each of the three eligible traineeship expenses, the following points may be considered:

Estimating trainee allowance. National legislation may be followed to set the level of allowance to be provided such as the national minimum wage. In countries in which allowances are not regarded as a salary or wage and that recognize traineeships as a training arrangement (compared to employment), there might be greater flexibility in setting allowances. In principle, allowances should always be fair and enable trainees to comfortably meet their daily subsistence needs such as transport, food, and shelter. There are

---

[9] The rationale for a gradual decreasing percentage is that it ensures that (i) trainee absorption capacity of projects is considered, (ii) traineeships remain a manageable project activity, and (iii) traineeship costs remain a moderate project expenditure.

[10] It should be noted that the same budget amount can generate differ traineeship targets in different countries given differences in labor costs between countries. Therefore, targets from one country are not transferable to other countries.

various ways to estimate traineeship allowances. For example, the national minimum wage may be taken as a benchmark, or in the absence of a national minimum wage trainees may receive a fraction of the wage (50%–80%) of entry-level staff (1–3 years' work experience) in a comparable occupation. In case the trainees receive a fraction of the wage, the lower allowance reflects the lower productivity of trainees. In addition, different construction occupations capture different salaries, which can affect traineeships allowance in different occupations. For example, welders tend to have higher earnings than bricklayers. With the various factors in mind, the guiding principle for setting allowances is fairness and subsistence.

Estimating workplace injury insurance costs. Types of work insurances offered for traineeships by national insurance markets as well as costs vary country by country. This should be determined in the design phase in consultation with the insurance market; TVET institutes may also be a source of information if traineeships are commonly used. In past projects insurance costs was around $10.[11]

Estimating PPE costs. PPE costs can vary. Differences in costs may reflect different consumer prices between countries and occupation-specific protection needs (e.g., welders require more PPE than painters). In past projects PPE costs ranged from $20 (Pakistan) to $50 (Mongolia). PPE can include boots, gloves, glasses, overalls, harnesses, and helmets. Generally, PPE estimates may include costs for safety helmets, overalls, and boots within product specifications that conform to common safety standards.

Companies do not need to provide a separate proposal for traineeships. The intention is that the Build4Skills initiative does not create additional bidding workload. Therefore, a separate technical proposal for traineeships is not mandatory. Instead, contractors may include traineeship-related information in their general proposal method statement with this requirement detailed in the contract specifications. Further traineeship implementation details can be provided by contractors during project implementation guided by the given traineeship specifications and steps 7–14 of the ADB *Build4Skills Handbook* that outline good practices in traineeship delivery.

BID EVALUATION AND CONTRACT AWARD

Specifications, pricing information, and any relevant sections of the contractor's proposal are included in the final contract between the parties. The contract creates a binding obligation on the contractor to deliver the Build4Skills traineeships throughout the life of the contract. Traineeship requirements and specifications may be highlighted to bidders during pre-bidding meetings and contract negotiation to align expectations between the employer and contractor. Following contract signature, any adjustments to the traineeship delivery will require the approval of both parties to the contract.

---

[11]   For example, in Pakistan in 2024 only a yearly work insurance was offered by the insurance market at a cost of about $10 per trainee.

CONTRACT MANAGEMENT—IMPLEMENTATION AND PERFORMANCE MONITORING

Employer monitors traineeship delivery. The employer tracks the delivery of traineeships by (i) requiring the contractor to submit progress reports (part of the traineeship contract specifications), (ii) verifying evidence of completion of traineeships submitted by contractors (part of the traineeship contract specifications), and (iii) collecting feedback from trainees for independent verification of traineeship delivery.

The terms of reference of employer staff and consultants shall include contract management tasks. The ADB *Build4Skills Handbook* recommends that the task of monitoring and tracking traineeships is included in the terms of reference (TORs) of various project consultants such as the supervision, contract management, and/or the community or gender engagement consultant. These TORs are typically part of project documents such as the project administration manual. TORs of those employer staff and consultants shall include tasks related to contract monitoring and management such as:

- review contractors' traineeship plans and verify proposed costing,
- ensure that progress reports are submitted,
- review progress reports and flag issues in terms of fulfilling specifications,
- verify evidence for the delivery of traineeships as submitted by contractors,
- communicate with contractors on any outstanding issues,
- coordinate disbursements related to traineeships, and
- collect trainee feedback.

Managing Provisional Sums and Disbursements

Use of traineeship provisional sum. When utilizing the provisional sum under the contract, the contractor will follow the general procedure set forth in the conditions of contract. In compliance with the specifications and provisional sum budget, when instructed by the employer, or their representative, the contractor shall provide a cost estimate to deliver the traineeships. Once approved by the employer, the contractor will be instructed to deliver the traineeships.

The subsequent disbursement phase focuses on the financial management of the contract, ensuring funds are released in a manner that supports the successful implementation of the traineeship program.

Managing disbursements. Disbursement will be based on the contractor's interim payment applications with the calculation shown under following milestones stated in Table 5—based on actual costs. Contractors must submit evidence to receive disbursements. The employer must verify the completeness and sufficiency of the submitted evidence and make a certification in the interim payment certificate.

Table 5: Disbursement Plan (Monthly Disbursements)

Milestone	Contractor to submit	Payment Condition	Disbursement
Traineeship preparation	• Proofs of workplace insurance • Proofs of handover of personal protective equipment • Proof of traineeship contracts	Engineer to certify disbursement when all criteria in traineeship quality checklists are met. (Preparation of traineeship plan and traineeship contracts are part of the overhead charges and profit)	Actual cost
Traineeship (implementation completion)	• Attendance logs • Proofs of allowance payment • Progress reports	Engineer to certify disbursements when all evidence is submitted and realistically document that traineeships have been successfully delivered	Actual cost

Source: Asian Development Bank.

Using the quality checklist (Table 6) to inform the approval of a first disbursement prior to the delivery of traineeships. Before traineeships can start, the employer should go through the quality checklist to ensure that all important preparatory issues, including occupational health and safety, have been addressed by contractors for the successful delivery of quality traineeships. It is recommended that the first traineeship-related disbursement to the contractor is made conditional on the successful completion of the criteria in the checklist through the employer. The contractor needs to submit evidence, such as a proof of workplace injury insurance and PPE handover and traineeship contracts (Table 5), to prove that the key quality criteria have been fulfilled (1–5 in Table 6). Evidence for quality criteria 6–10 in Table 6 may not be readily available. In these cases, contractors are required to attest and explain to the employer, in a formal communication, that the criteria have been planned for and given due consideration. For example, the contractor may outline how transport and food provisions for trainees will be addressed. The employer then needs to affirm that the contractor has outlined and communicated that those criteria have been satisfactorily considered and addressed.

Evidence for traineeship completion to guide final disbursement. After the delivery of traineeships, contractors shall submit proof of successful delivery and request for disbursements. Proofs of completion include attendance logs, proof of allowance handover, and progress reports (Table 5). The employer verifies that traineeships have successfully taken place to certify the disbursement. To verify the authenticity of evidence submitted the employer may compare trainee signature in different documents such as traineeship contracts and attendance log, and progress reports may include images.

Table 6: Build4Skills Quality Checklist Before Traineeship Start

	Criteria	Evidence	Check
1	Traineeship contracts have been signed by all stakeholders including students or their legal guardians	Traineeship contract	
2	All trainees have received occupational health and safety training	Participant list	
3	All trainees have received personal protective equipment as required	PPE handover list	
4	All trainees have a workplace injury insurance for the traineeship period	Proof of insurance	
5	The terms of how and when trainees receive their stipends are clearly outlined	May be indicated in traineeship contract	
6	Contractors have assigned an on-site instructor for trainees	May be outlined and specified either in the traineeship contract, traineeship plan, or other formal communication (e.g., explanation note)	
7	Trainees have been fully briefed about traineeships, their responsibilities, and other issues		
8	Transport and food provisions for trainees have been considered and addressed		
9	For female trainees, considerations for a gender-sensitive traineeship environment have been made		
10	For underage trainees, appropriate considerations and measures have been made		

PPE = personal protective equipment.
Source: Asian Development Bank.

Verify Quality of Traineeship Delivery in Detail

Verifying traineeship completion and quality through trainee evaluation forms. In addition to the evidence submitted by the contractor, the employer is encouraged to collect feedback directly from trainees immediately after the completion of the traineeship through a trainee evaluation form. The purpose of the evaluation is for the employer to independently verify that contractors have met traineeship contract specifications regarding (i) providing sufficient supervision, (ii) ensuring occupational health and safety, (iii) paying trainee stipends, and (iv) employing trainees in relevant technical work areas. A template for trainee evaluation is outlined in Appendix 3. If the results of the evaluation do not confirm the delivery of traineeships according to specifications, the employers may follow up with the contractor for clarification and corrective actions.

In addition, the results of the trainee evaluation are recommended to be included in the contractor traineeship performance certificate, that employers may provide to contractors to certify corporate social responsibility (step 15 in the *Build4Skills Handbook*). The contractor traineeship certificate of recognition is optional and unrelated to disbursements.

Good practices when collecting trainee feedback. The employer collects trainee feedback at the end of traineeships. The contractor cannot collect the feedback due to a conflict of interest. A good practice is to require trainees to submit the evaluation form before they receive their traineeship certificate of completion. A template evaluation form is outlined in Appendix 3. The form includes five questions related to traineeship delivery quality that trainees are requested to answer on a four-point Linkert scale (totally agree, agree, disagree, totally disagree). The use of a Linkert scale ensures that replies are uniform and provide clear evaluative responses.

Identifying noncompliance with traineeship specifications. Based on the evidence, or the lack of it, the employer may determine that traineeships were not delivered according to specifications and therefore are noncompliant. Possible noncompliance in key traineeship requirements is outlined and defined in Table 7, which may guide the employer to identify noncompliance. It is recommended that the employer raises issues of noncompliance to contractors and requests corrective actions in future traineeships and potentially retroactively if appropriate.

Table 7: Definitions of Noncompliance for Key Traineeship Specifications

Area	Recommended Traineeships Specification	Definition of Noncompliance	Verification Source
General delivery	Contractors must provide traineeship opportunities.	If the traineeship target is not met, allowing for a deviation by 10%.[a]	• Attendance log • Progress report • Traineeship contracts
Duration	Traineeships must be 6 weeks or longer.	If traineeships are shorter than 6 weeks.	• Traineeship contract • Evaluation form
Work areas	Traineeships must consistently[b] take place in technical work areas related to construction and engineering professions.	If trainees spent 20% (or more) of their traineeship time on nontechnical tasks or jobs (such as security guard, food services, or office clerk).	• Traineeship contract • Evaluation form
Supervision	Traineeships are to be supervised by contractor staff.	If trainees were not supervised[c] by contractor staff.	• Evaluation form
Occupational and Health and Safety (OHS)	Contractors must ensure that trainees receive OHS training prior to the traineeship.	If the contractor cannot provide evidence that trainees received OHS instructions.	• Signed participants list of OHS training
Personal Protective Equipment (PPE)	Contractors must ensure that trainees have PPE as required for the tasks performed during traineeship.	If the contractor cannot provide evidence that trainees received appropriate PPE.	• Signed PPE handover list
Traineeship allowance	Contractor must remunerate trainees with an appropriate allowance.	If the contractor cannot provide evidence that trainees received an appropriate[d] traineeship allowance.	• Allowance payment slip

[a] The contractor shall be allowed to explain noncompliance, for example, in some cases trainees may not show up for traineeships due to various reasons.
[b] "Consistently" may be defined as 4 out of 5 working days or 75% of daily working hours spent on technical tasks.
[c] Supervision includes trainees participating in daily construction team briefings that discuss tasks of the day, and technical staff explaining to trainees how to perform tasks in regular intervals (2–3 times per week).
[d] An appropriate allowance is one that is sufficient to cover daily travel and food expenses of an individual and has no significant gap to minimum wage or average salaries of comparable junior staff. Ideally it is documented in the traineeship contract.

Source: Asian Development Bank.

APPENDIX 1
Traineeship Specifications to Be Included in Bidding Documents

Traineeship provision. The Contractor must provide on-the-job traineeships to XX trainees, for students from vocational and technical training institutes. The training must fulfill the following conditions:

- Traineeships last at minimum for 6 weeks.

- Trainees must learn on the job directly on the construction site.

- Trainees must be assigned to technical works that match their qualification background. Technical work areas include but are not limited to, welders, bricklayers, joiners, electricians, painters, pipefitters, roofers, ironworkers, cement workers, solar panel installers, and other civil engineering-related professions.

- Trainees must be supervised by an instructor who regularly instructs trainees on performing tasks and oversees their general welfare. Regular instructions refer to the practice of instructing trainees when they are performing tasks that are new to them and providing feedback at minimum two times per week. It may also include job-shadowing.

- Trainees must always wear appropriate personal protective equipment (PPE) when on the construction site.

- Trainees must be work insured for the duration of the traineeship.

- Contractors shall provide the same occupational health and safety conditions to trainees as to any other construction workers engaged on the construction sites, in line with applicable safeguards and national regulations.

The Contractor shall fulfill the following specifications when planning for traineeships, implementing traineeships, and after traineeships. The Contractor may use the ADB Build4Skills Handbook including its templates available on the ADB website, as an additional implementation support guide.

Arranging Traineeships

Submit traineeship plan. Ten weeks prior to the planned implementation date of the first traineeship batch, the Contractor shall provide a high-level traineeship plan that includes the following information:

- Overview in which job areas traineeships will take place, and the number of trainees per job area. Only technical construction professions are permissible as job areas which include but are not limited to, welders, bricklayers, joiners, electrician, painters, pipefitters, roofers, ironworkers, cement workers, solar panel installers, and other civil engineering-related professions.

- Traineeship schedule for the contract duration.

- Short description of which workplace injury insurance and PPE will be provided to trainees.

- Cost plan outlining trainee costs for (i) trainee stipend, (ii) insurance costs, (iii) personal protective gear (other costs are not permissible).

- Short description of specific opportunities for female trainees on the construction site.

- List of assigned trainee instructors, including name and role of contractor staff.

- Key information on technical and vocational education and training (TVET) schools from where trainees will be recruited.

Coordinate with TVET institute in student selection. The Contractor is responsible for informing partner TVET institutes about upcoming traineeship needs and requests TVET institutes to identify and nominate students for traineeships. The Contractor shall provide full information about the traineeship conditions, schedule, and work areas to enable TVET institutes to select students that are available and have qualifications that match the traineeship work areas.

Sign traineeship contracts. The Contractor must sign traineeship contracts with trainees to formalize traineeships. All signed traineeship contracts must be shared with the employer before the start of the traineeships. The traineeship contract must at minimum outline the following points, but may include additional information:

- Trainee name, trainee contact information, parents contact information (if underaged)
- Trainee's TVET school and head teacher name and contact information
- Dates of traineeship and daily traineeships hours
- Location of traineeship site
- Trainee allowance and payment procedure
- Trainee PPE, workplace injury insurance arrangement and other health and safety considerations
- Traineeship work area
- Trainee responsibilities
- Contractor responsibilities
- TVET institute responsibilities (if applicable)

Set a fair traineeship allowance. The Contractor must provide trainees with a fair traineeship allowance. A fair traineeship allowance is either an allowance aligned with the national or sectoral minimum wage, or an allowance that enables trainees to meet their daily subsistence needs such as transport, food, and shelter and is not lower than 60% of the salary of entry-level skilled worker in a comparable occupation. Fairness and subsistence are guiding principles for setting fair traineeship allowances. The Contractor shall confirm the allowance to be paid to trainees as part of their proposal to deliver the traineeships.

Arrange trainee workplace injury insurance. Before the start of the traineeship, the Contractor must ensure that trainees are insured against injury and harm on the construction site. Proof of insurance issued by the insurance company must be shared with the employer prior to the start of traineeships. The proof of insurance must clearly state (i) trainee's name, (ii) insurance duration, (iii) insurance type and coverage, (iv) name of insurance issuer. It must be a document issued by the insurer.

Handover PPE. Prior to the start of the traineeship, the Contractor must ensure that trainees have received PPE as needed for a given traineeship. Proof of handover of PPE to trainees must be shared with the employer before traineeships begin. The proof must state:

    (i)   Name of all PPE items handed over

    (ii)   Handover date and location

    (iii) Trainee name and trainee signature receiving the PPE

    (iv) Name and signature of contractor staff handing over PPE

Provide occupational health and safety instructions. Before the start of traineeships, the Contractor must provide occupational and health and safety (OHS) instructions to trainees as is required for any other worker working on the give project's construction site in line with applicable laws and civil works contractual stipulations. The Contractor must provide proof that OHS has been completed in form of a training participant list that includes the following information:

    (i)   Date and location of training

    (ii)   Name of training provided

    (iii) Name of person delivering training

    (iv) Name of trainee receiving training and trainee signature

Delivering Traineeships

Oversee traineeship attendance and sign work daily. The Contractor shall track the attendance of each trainee through an attendance log that will be submitted to the employer at the end of traineeships. Each attendance log must be signed by a company staff and the respective trainee. The Contractor shall inform TVET schools in case trainees have regularly unexcused absences or do not follow traineeship tasks.

Submit progress reports. The Contractor must submit progress reports every 6 months detailing the progress of the traineeship program, including the following information:

- Total number of trainees trained since the start of project
- Short description of traineeship activities (1–2 pages)
- Appendix 1: List of trainees (name, contact detail, work area, traineeship time frame, name of TVET institutes where enrolled)
- Appendix 2: Attendance log

After Traineeship Completion

Provide reference letter to trainees. At the completion of traineeships, the Contractor shall provide trainees with a reference letter (or similar) that confirms the trainee's work engagement. The reference letter shall attest that a given trainee has completed a traineeship at the contractor and include at minimum the following information:

- Name of trainee
- Name of contractor
- Duration of traineeship
- Short description of work area and tasks trainee has worked on
- Name of the Asian Development Bank-supported project

Attend certificate of participation award ceremony. Representatives of the Contractor shall make time to participate in trainee award ceremonies organized by TVET institutes and other project stakeholders.

Evidence for traineeship delivery. When submitting invoices related to expenses of traineeships, the Contractor must provide the following documents to the employer as evidence that traineeships have been successfully delivered:

- Attendance log for each trainee
- Allowance payment slip including the following information, (i) allowance amount paid to trainee, (ii) payment date and location, (iii) trainee name and trainee signature receiving the allowance, (iv) name and signature of person performing payment
- Progress report
- Traineeship contracts

Feedback collection through employer. The Contractor agrees that the employer may contact trainees and collect feedback from trainees regarding their traineeship experience.

Template for Market Survey for Traineeships

Introduction

Welcome to our survey on the Build4Skills approach in infrastructure projects. Your input is crucial for advancing our initiative that integrates skill development into infrastructure development, going beyond traditional project outcomes to foster workforce upskilling and community development.

Survey Purpose. This survey aims to gauge the readiness and capacity of our partners to implement the Build4Skills approach, identifying areas for support and improvement to enhance project and societal outcomes.

Build4Skills Approach. Build4Skills embeds training, mentorship, and on-the-job learning within infrastructure projects, aiming to build human capital, addressing skill gaps, and boosting local employment opportunities.

Importance. By embedding the Build4Skills approach, we aim to transform infrastructure projects into platforms for sustainable development, directly contributing to economic growth and community resilience.

Confidentiality. Rest assured, your responses will remain confidential and will be used exclusively to refine and promote the Build4Skills approach in our projects, aligning infrastructure development with skills development and economic empowerment.

Thank you for contributing to this pivotal initiative. Your insights are invaluable in shaping a more inclusive and sustainable future in infrastructure development.

If you need any further information, please contact [*Project Implementation Unit contact name and email address*]

Supplier information

1. Company name and contact details.

2. Years of operation in the infrastructure sector.

3. Size of the company (e.g., number of employees).

Experience with traineeships

1. Have you previously implemented traineeship or apprenticeship programs? (Yes/No)

2. If yes, provide details on the scope of the traineeship, location, number of trainees, duration, and sectors.

3. Have you partnered with educational institutions or training centers to deliver apprenticeships? If yes, briefly explain.

Capabilities for delivering traineeships

1. Do you have company staff that are assigned for on-the-job training? If yes, do they have any pedagogical qualifications?

2. Do you have any capacity to deliver occupational health and safety training to trainees? If yes, please describe.

3. Do you have any staff in the human resource department that is assigned to manage apprenticeships (or similar)?

Commitment to Build4Skills objectives

1. On a scale of 1 to 5, rate your interest in participating in B4S traineeships within future projects (*1 being no interest, 5 being very interested*).

2. How willing are you to collaborate on developing training programs with procuring entities or training institutions? (*Options: Very willing; Willing; Somewhat willing; Not willing*)

Feedback and suggestions

1. Please provide suggestions on how the procurement process can better support the integration of traineeships.

2. Please provide any additional comments or feedback on the market survey

Trainee Evaluation Form Template

1. Each trainee must fill out this form providing truthful information.
2. Individual responses will not be shared with contractors.
3. Do not write your name on the form. The feedback is anonymous.

Instructions: *Please respond to the following questions in writing.*

Basic information	Answer
Today's date dd/mm/yyyy	
Where did your traineeship take place? *City*	
Which contractor did you work for? *Name of contractor*	
In which occupation did you complete the traineeship? *Name of occupation*	
Which training institute / school are you attending? *Name of school or TVET institute*	

Instruction: *Please indicate your level of agreement with the following 5 statements by drawing a circle around the answer, like the example in blue.*

Example   *This traineeship form is easy to fill out*   Strongly agree   *Agree*   *Disagree*   Strongly disagree

continued on next page

Table continued

Statement 1: In my traineeship, I worked on tasks that matched my education background.	Strongly agree	Agree	Disagree	Strongly disagree
Statement 2: At least once a week, an instructor (e.g., company staff) gave me instructions that helped me to perform tasks effectively.	Strongly agree	Agree	Disagree	Strongly disagree
Statement 3: Instructors (e.g., company staff) ensured that I always followed safe working practices and conditions.	Strongly agree	Agree	Disagree	Strongly disagree
Statement 4: I received a traineeship allowance/ stipend as agreed in the traineeship contract.	Strongly agree	Agree	Disagree	Strongly disagree
Statement 5: The traineeship has significantly improved my skills and knowledge.	Strongly agree	Agree	Disagree	Strongly disagree

If you want to share anything else, please write it in the box below (optional):

You are done. Please submit the form. Thank you for filling out the form.

9789292709037